M000227951

Five
Means
of Grace

Experience God's Love
the Wesleyan Way

Leader Guide

Elaine A. Heath

Abingdon Press™

Nashville

FIVE MEANS OF GRACE LEADER GUIDE:
EXPERIENCE GOD'S LOVE THE WESLEYAN WAY

Copyright © 2017 by Abingdon Press

All rights reserved.

No part of this work may be reproduced or transmitted in any form or by any means, electronic or mechanical, including photocopying and recording, or by any information storage or retrieval system, except as may be expressly permitted by the 1976 Copyright Act or in writing from the publisher. Requests for permission should be addressed in writing to Permissions, The United Methodist Publishing House, 2222 Rosa L. Parks Blvd., PO Box 280988, Nashville, TN 37228-0988, or e-mailed to permissions@ umpublishing.org.

This book is printed on acid-free paper.

ISBN: 978-1-5018-3555-1

Scripture quotations unless noted otherwise are from the Common English Bible. Copyright © 2011 by the Common English Bible. All rights reserved. Used by permission. www.CommonEnglishBible.com.

17 18 19 20 21 22 23 24 25 26—10 9 8 7 6 5 4 3 2 1

MANUFACTURED IN THE UNITED STATES OF AMERICA

Contents

How to Use This Leader Guide

Welcome to *Five Means of Grace*! As a facilitator, you play a key role in the weekly classroom sessions, which are a critical component of the study's overall experience. Your guidance will shape the interactions between participants and nurture the impact that this study has on their lives.

The Goal and Scope of *Five Means of Grace*

This study will guide your participants in a discovery of the essential practices for experiencing God's love the Wesleyan way, based on professor Elaine A. Heath's book called *Five Means of Grace*. She provides an in-depth study from John Wesley's published works about a shared Christian life together, which is possible through five indispensable spiritual practices. We experience and pass along God's grace through the following means:

1. Prayer

2. Searching the Scriptures

3. The Lord's Supper

4. Fasting

5. Christian Conferencing

This is a six-week study that begins with a general overview of Christian spiritual practices, which Wesley and countless Christians believe to be the channels for knowing God's love. Each of the following five weeks investigates each of the means more fully. By the end of this study, participants will be able to:

- articulate the five essential "means of grace";

- ground their understanding of the five means in the Bible and Wesleyan theology;

- identify common barriers to living out each of the five means; and

- renew their commitment to practicing the five means in service to others for the glory of God.

The Role of Facilitator

You need not be a formally trained Wesleyan scholar with profound biblical understanding in order to succeed as a facilitator. You need only the following attributes to do your work well:

Be a Learner: You are, first and foremost, a fellow participant on this journey. As you read the weekly material, you will be tempted to do so exclusively through the lens of a facilitator. Instead, allow yourself to be as transformed and inspired by these indispensable practices as you hope your participants will be. Cultivate a curiosity and openness to meanings that are important to you, and others will draw from your enthusiasm.

Be a Tour Guide: You don't need to be a resident expert on every biblical and theological matter that your group will discuss. Instead, like a docent in a museum, your job will simply be to direct their attention to aspects of our Wesleyan heritage and the Christian faith that are important for them to notice. You will guide conversations with structured questions designed to draw their interest and elicit their input.

Be Prepared: The success of the classroom experience is directly related to your level of preparedness before each session. By using the material in this leader's guide, familiarize yourself with the learning objectives and key concepts for each week, carefully craft the questions that will spur conversation in your group, and structure both the time and the setting to be most conducive to learning.

Be Attentive to Stories: There is an easy tendency in a small-group study like this one to get completely caught up in conversations about theology and biblical interpretation. Sometimes, however, the most effective way to deepen our understanding is through storytelling. Allow and encourage people to tell their own stories, modeling for them the power of storytelling by being vulnerable enough to do so yourself. Remember that a key to your group's success will be training people to listen to stories: not just the stories they share with others but the grand, unfolding story of God's love found in Scripture.

The Classroom Experience

Each *Five Means of Grace* session follows the same essential structure, with some variations from week to week. The recurring sections are introduced here. The total suggested class length for each session is fifty-five minutes.

GATHERING (5 Minutes)

The opening questions of this segment are based on a reading of a passage in the book and help focus the group on the general theme of the session ahead.

REFLECTIONS ON THE READING (10 to 15 Minutes)

This segment helps participants dig deeply into the central theme of the session by sharing discoveries from the reading and investigating key concepts together. Participation is often structured in pairs or small groups in order to maximize sharing and encourage discussion from those who may be initially reluctant.

VIDEO SEGMENT (15 Minutes)

The video features Elaine A. Heath, dean of the divinity school at Duke University, a professor of missional and pastoral theology, and author of *Five Means of Grace*. Her conversation partner is Joerg Rieger, professor of theology and Methodist studies at Vanderbilt University. Participants will be able to gain wisdom from their personal reflections on the weekly theme, prompting their own ideas and questions.

VIDEO DISCUSSION QUESTIONS (10 to 15 Minutes)

These questions prompt the participants to reflect on Elaine Heath's words in the context of their own discoveries.

LOOKING AHEAD AND CLOSING PRAYER (5 Minutes)

The final segment briefly introduces the particular means of grace for the forthcoming week. Each session then closes with a time for the sharing of prayer requests and concerns, encouraging participants to write down each other's needs and remember them in the upcoming week.

The Basic Needs of a Small Group

Everyone has essential needs that emerge from three categories. To ensure a fruitful, healthy classroom experience for your participants, pay attention to these basic necessities:

PHYSICAL NEEDS: "Am I Safe and Comfortable?"

People have fundamental physical needs that must be addressed in order for them to maintain focus and attention. To meet these needs, address the following:

- Temperature: Set the thermostat in the room at a comfortable level.

- Comfort: Allow food, drinks, bathroom breaks, and time to stand up and stretch.

- Punctuality: Honor the time commitments people are making to the study by starting and ending each session promptly. When time is up, even if it is in the middle of a conversation, give people permission to leave if they need to, being particularly attentive to child care needs and nursery volunteers.

- Minimal Distractions: Reduce distracting outside noises. Invite people to silence their cell phones at the start of each session and to refrain from texting.

EMOTIONAL NEEDS: *"Who Is Around Me? Can I Trust Them?"*

For people to feel fully secure, they need to be comfortable with those around them. To meet these needs, address the following:

- Names: Learn people's names right away, say their names to them often, and welcome them personally when they arrive.

- Chairs: Arrange the chairs in the room to suggest equality—no chairs higher, more comfortable, or more prominently placed than others.

- Prayer: Pray for your participants, even (and especially) before they meet for the first time. Always allow time for the sharing of joys and concerns at the conclusion of each session, and encourage people to share the task of offering the closing prayer.

- Confidentiality: Remind people often that what is shared during each session must remain kept to themselves.

- Healthy Disagreement: It is likely that people will offer contradictory points of view. Don't shy away from conflict, as sometimes those discussions will elicit opportunities for growth. However, don't let those disagreements become personal.

MENTAL NEEDS: *"Why Am I Here? What's the Point?"*

Finally, people need to know that the time they invest into this experience will be well spent. To be certain they can gauge the merits and progress of this process, address the following:

- Main Point: Share with the group the main points of each session that will direct their time and energies.

- Preparation: Model for them the benefits of being prepared by reading all the material in advance and keeping the discussions moving forward.

- Questions: Carefully construct the questions you will ask the group to discuss, tailoring them to the interests and dynamics of the group. Use "open-ended" questions that require more than simple responses from participants.

- Listening: Though you are a participant and are free to offer your own insights, model healthy conversation by being a good listener. The ideal ratio of talking/listening for a facilitator is 20/80.

- Enthusiasm: Share your excitement and encourage participation by completing all the assigned work yourself.

Helpful Hints

Because every group comprises different people, your class may have its own particular set of dynamics and challenges. The following are some helpful tips to help your group succeed:

The ideal class size. Groups of eight to twelve people are an ideal size. Classes that are larger than twelve make it too easy for people to feel anonymous and even miss classes without being noticed. Large groups often take longer to form the kinds of relationships that are critical to meaningful small group study. Groups smaller than eight can lack the kind of diversity of background and opinion that enhance the richness of the experience.

What to do when a participant talks too much. When you sense that someone is commanding too much of the discussion, carefully determine whether or not that person is being a detriment to the group process. Some people, after all, have a personality that necessitates speaking in order to think. But if you discern that correction is necessary for the benefit of the class, first try some nonverbal cues. Avoid making eye contact with that person when you ask a question of the group. Break the group into smaller discussion groups in order to minimize the person's effect on the whole group. Also try some verbal cues: remind people after you ask certain questions to keep answers brief. Ask other people in the group for their response. Of course, if necessary, address the concern privately with an individual outside of class, thanking that person for his or her contributions and asking for his or her assistance in eliciting discussion from others in the group.

What to do when a participant talks too little. There are individuals who require time to process their own thoughts before they verbalize them. Others are more introverted, shying away from talking in front of a large group. Again, manage eye contact to look directly at those who appear reluctant to talk. Breaking the group into pairs encourages everyone to share their opinions. Do refrain, however, from putting people on the spot. No one should feel coerced into speaking when he or she is uncomfortable. And when quieter people do choose to speak their thoughts in front of the whole group, praise them for their contribution without sounding patronizing.

Don't be afraid of silence. Sometimes, when you ask a question, there will be prolonged periods of silence in the group. You will be tempted to interrupt that silence with your own answers and insights, move quickly to another question, or call out people directly for their response. Instead, feel free to sit in that silence, trusting that people are sorting out their own answers and struggling in a healthy way. Rather than breaking that silence with your own answers, a good alternative is to break the class into smaller groups to discuss the question, making it less threatening for folks to develop their own responses verbally.

Stay on track. Inevitably, topics of conversation will emerge from your group that aren't central to the main points of the session. Use your best judgment in discerning which discussions are more diversionary and less helpful. Gently return the conversation back to the central ideas and, if need be, offer opportunities for interested folks to continue those conversations after class.

Session 1

The Means of Grace Are Spiritual Practices

INTRODUCTION

A prodigy is someone with extraordinary talent who seems to instantly pick up a skill or craft that takes others a long time to learn or master. However, even prodigies realize they need to practice, and most people have also experienced what it means to learn a set of practices in order to do a job, play a musical instrument, or enjoy a sport.

Grace in Christian language is properly understood as an unmerited gift from God, freely available to all despite our human shortcomings and flaws. Nothing we can do or say will earn God's faithful love and grace. Yet to stay in love with God—"to attend to God's ordinances"— John Wesley taught all Christians that five practices are indispensable channels for experiencing (not earning) God's grace.

This opening session will help your class

1. explore the concept of grace and why it is a foundational topic for spiritual growth;

2. offer initial impressions of the five means of grace as a baseline for understanding; and

3. commit together to create an environment of support, prayer, and trust.

GATHERING (5 Minutes)

Invite participants to listen as you read aloud the following lines from Charles Wesley's twenty-three-stanza hymn "The Means of Grace." Invite students to reflect silently on the words for two minutes. After the silence, have them turn to a person next to them to share what words, phrases, or ideas resonate with them.

> Long have I seemed to serve you, Lord,
>   with unavailing pain;
> Fasted and prayed and read your word,
>   and heard it preached in vain.
>
> Oft did I with your assembly join,
>   and near your altar drew;
> A form of godliness was mine,
>   the power I never knew.
>
> To please you thus, at length I see,
>   vainly I hoped and strove:
> For what are outward things to you,
>   unless they spring from love?
> (*A Collection of Hymns for the Use of the People Called Methodists*, no. 91, adapted)

This hymn was written in 1740 as a response to a few early Methodists who questioned the value of worship, Holy Communion, and other means of grace for stimulating or deepening Christian faith. Ask a participant to open the session with a word of prayer.

REFLECTIONS ON THE READING (10 Minutes)

Have the class brainstorm a list of the kinds of groups they are involved in outside the church. That list might include civic organizations, service clubs, recreational sports leagues, work teams, and so on. After the class has come up with that list, have them explore more deeply one or two of the groups on the list. Write up a list of practices that are necessary for each member of the group. For example, for a sports team practices might include "eye-hand coordination" or "blocking and tackling."

As a class, have everyone reflect on the question, "How does being part of a group shape the practices for the individual members of that group?" Then make the connection to the Christian church. Tell the class that for Methodists there are five means of grace (or five channels for God's grace) that help Christians stay in love with God:

1. Prayer

2. Searching the Scriptures

3. The Lord's Supper

4. Fasting

5. Christian Conferencing

VIDEO SEGMENT (15 Minutes)

Video segment featuring Elaine A. Heath, author of *Five Means of Grace*, in conversation with theology professor Joerg Rieger.

VIDEO DISCUSSION QUESTIONS (10 Minutes)

1. What did you hear? Do you have any stories from your childhood or youth in which someone became God's grace to you? Were these mountaintop experiences or everyday graces?

15

2. If spiritual practices (prayer, searching the Scriptures, the Lord's Supper, fasting, and Christian conferencing) are really about nurturing our relationship with God, then what are some ways we can be open to the Holy Spirit when we do these things?

3. When we open up to God we discover God's heart for the world. What are some of the real places grace might be sending you and your church?

4. What would a new encounter with God over the next six weeks mean in your life? Your friends' and family's lives?

THE JOURNEY AHEAD (10 Minutes)

A. *The Five Means*

Have the class refer again to the list of five means of grace that will guide these sessions ahead. As a group, discuss each of the five means, and ask people to share their initial understanding of what that channel means for experiencing God's grace.

- What does it mean, for example, to pray?
- Why is this one of the five identified as important or indispensable?
- What questions do you have about this means of grace?

B. *Experiencing God's Love in This Group*

Together, come up with a list of ground rules that will define this group's time together. What can participants expect from each other in relation to each of the following commitments:

16

- being prepared for each session

- listening and contributing to each session

- honoring differences

- resolving conflict

- encouraging honesty and protecting confidentiality

- praying for each other

- being punctual and honoring each other's time

- creating an atmosphere of joy, love, and laughter

After the class comes up with these shared values, have the list printed and displayed for all future sessions. Class members might even choose to sign the list to ritually commit to sharing those values.

LOOKING AHEAD AND CLOSING PRAYER (5 Minutes)

Have the class share joys and prayer concerns, and invite them to be in prayer for each other over the upcoming week. Invite someone to close in prayer.

Session 2

One: Prayer

INTRODUCTION

Prayer is an indispensable means for experiencing God's love. John Wesley includes it in his other foundational teachings about the three simple rules for Methodists, the five characteristics or marks of a Methodist, and the faithful covenant promise that can restore and refresh a dry spirit. Apart from regular communication with God, personally and corporately, it's not possible to sustain a relationship.

This session will help your class

1. start with prayer rather than doctrine, because prayer is involved in every means of grace;

2. learn why prayer and vulnerability are necessary to persist through inevitable suffering; and

3. discover creative prayer resources.

GATHERING (5 Minutes)

Invite participants to read in unison from Psalm 130:1-2 (CEB):

I cry out to you from the depths, LORD—
my Lord, listen to my voice!
Let your ears pay close attention to my request for mercy!

Invite students to reflect silently on those words for a minute. Then read the following stanza of a poem Charles Wesley wrote in 1739 on the psalmist's cry for help, which is a lament:

Out of the depth of self-despair,
   To thee, O Lord, I cry;
My misery mark, attend my prayer,
   And bring salvation nigh.
(*A Collection of Hymns for the Use of the People Called Methodists*, no. 768)

Ask a participant to open the session with a word of prayer for someone or some people who are facing very deep trouble in our world.

REFLECTIONS ON THE READING (10 Minutes)

Tell participants that prayer is "gazing into the face of Jesus who gazes back with infinite love." Elaine Heath reminds us that it's not possible for God to lose or diminish God's love for each of us. But we can safely let down our guard—a guard that keeps God at a distance—through vulnerability, trust, and honesty. "Prayer is the very breath of God, breathing life into us, opening us to who God is, to who we are, and to this world that God loves."

Invite the class to work together to come up with a list of various types of prayer. Guide the class to think about descriptors such as "lament" (or "cry for help"), "thanksgiving," "praise," "intercession," and so forth.

VIDEO SEGMENT (15 Minutes)

Video segment featuring Elaine A. Heath, author of *Five Means of Grace*, in conversation with theology professor Joerg Rieger.

VIDEO DISCUSSION QUESTIONS
(10 Minutes)

1. Recall the advice of Elaine Heath's mentor: Don't
   teach new believers doctrine—first teach them how
   to pray [and] as they experience that love over time
   they will have what they need to discern good and bad
   theology. Do you agree? Why or why not? How might
   prayer give access to things "deeper" than doctrine?

2. In addition to listening for God's voice in Scripture
   and hymns, Joerg and Elaine say that prayer is listening to God's voice in the experiences of those who suffer oppression and deprivation. How is Jesus's heart,
   experience, and call found in the cries of those who
   suffer (see Matt 25:31-46)?

3. Is there a connection between being honest—telling the truth in prayer—and aligning ourselves with
   God and God's mission/work in the world? How are
   the Psalms a good example of this kind of real-world
   honesty?

4. Heath and Rieger discuss prayer as a struggle to know
   God and recognize what God wants us to do. How
   can prayer be a part of a shared struggle to see what is
   true and how God wants us to live and love?

REFLECTIONS ON SCRIPTURE
(10 Minutes)

Invite the class to recite the Lord's Prayer, and then read aloud the
version from the Common English Bible in Matthew 6:9-13:

Our Father who is in heaven,
uphold the holiness of your name.
Bring in your kingdom
so that your will is done on earth as it's done in heaven.
Give us the bread we need for today.
Forgive us for the ways we have wronged you,
just as we also forgive those who have wronged us.
And don't lead us into temptation,
but rescue us from the evil one.

Have the class reflect together on barriers that prevent us from praying. What barriers are the most difficult to overcome? Ask, "Do you tend to practice one kind of prayer? What are some resources that might introduce you to other creative forms of communication with God?" (If possible, bring some examples of prayer helps, such as hymnals, books of prayers, devotional guides, daily orders for morning and evening prayer, and so forth.)

LOOKING AHEAD AND CLOSING PRAYER (5 Minutes)

Have the class share joys and prayer concerns, and invite them to be in prayer for each other over the coming week. Have each person choose someone in the group to pray for during the next week. Don't identify the person in class, but encourage each participant to bring a brief note next week to give to the person held up in prayer. So that nobody is left out, the leader should pray by name and bring a note for each person in the group. Invite someone to close this session in prayer.

Two: Searching the Scriptures

INTRODUCTION

Reading the Bible is for the explicit purpose of Christian transformation. Scripture tells us that we need to change our hearts and lives (the Greek concept *metanoia*). The stories, prayers, and commandments show us how this transformation happens over and over again.

Especially during a crisis, a well-formed Christian instinctively turns to Scripture for grace, wisdom, and guidance. This session will help your class determine

1. the conditions under which a person can "search the Scriptures" and encounter therein the living God;

2. apparent obstacles to seeing and hearing God through Scripture when we do read the Bible; and

3. how one goes about reading the Bible so that scriptures come to mind helpfully when we need them.

GATHERING (5 Minutes)

Charles Wesley's hymns and poems drew from thousands of images and phrases in Scripture. Invite participants to suggest favorite hymns or praise songs that draw directly from Scripture.

Ask a participant to open the session with a word of prayer or, if courageous, sing together the first stanza of "And Can It Be that I Should Gain" by Charles Wesley (*The United Methodist Hymnal*, no. 363).

And can it be that I should gain
    an interest in the Savior's blood!
Died he for me? who caused his pain!
    For me? who him to death pursued?
Amazing love! How can it be,
    that thou, my God, shouldst die for me?
Amazing love! How can it be
    that thou, my God, shouldst die for me?

REFLECTIONS ON THE READING (10 Minutes)

Invite participants to share an experience when a passage from Scripture or a sermon on a Bible passage changed their heart or mind about a particular problem or crisis. Look for examples of comfort as well as an encounter with the living and awesome God.

Next invite participants who are willing to share how the Bible was or can be used inappropriately to judge or oppress the faith of others. Acknowledge that the Bible is sometimes used as a weapon to cause harm, but steer the conversation toward the right ways to search the Scriptures so that God's grace is experienced through love. Before playing the video, briefly discuss the following questions:

1. If reading the Bible is a means of grace, how often should a Christian search the Scriptures?

2. What are some annoying barriers that get in the way of searching the Scriptures?

VIDEO SEGMENT (15 Minutes)

Video segment featuring Elaine A. Heath, author of *Five Means of Grace*, in conversation with theology professor Joerg Rieger.

VIDEO DISCUSSION QUESTIONS (10 Minutes)

1. Has the Bible been a go-to place to recognize God's call for you? What do you think about the "four scopes" strategy for searching the Scriptures?

2. What might be obstacles to seeing and hearing God through Scripture when we do read the Bible?

3. How can reading the Bible together help us experience grace and realign our lives with God's purposes?

REFLECTIONS ON SCRIPTURE (10 Minutes)

Use the steps of *Lectio Divina* (repeated and adapted here from pp. 31–33 in *Five Means of Grace*) to pray, that is *search*, the Scriptures with John 5:1-15. Read the text aloud to the group more than once and share with each other what you experience.

Lectio Divina has four movements, which don't always follow in the sequence set forth below. The reading is done with an orientation toward listening to the Holy Spirit who may speak through the text. This principle is in keeping with the Confession that guided Wesley, that the Bible reveals the word of God. To prepare for reading one should quiet oneself and open one's heart to the Holy Spirit in readiness for whatever may be given. The intention is to hear whatever the Holy Spirit may say through the text and to pray with it and then live into it in whatever ways God asks.

25

Reading is the first movement. Read through John 5:1-15 slowly, at least twice. As the reader moves slowly in a listening manner through the text, he or she may sense a phrase, word, sentence, or concept emerging from the text, drawing the reader's attention. At that point the reader should pause. As Wesley instructs in his preface to the *Explanatory Notes upon the Old Testament*, the pause allows the text to examine the reader.

This pause is the second movement of *Lectio*: *meditation*. In this part, the reader reflects on the word, image, or phrase that surfaced from the reading. It is time for a deeper listening to what God wants to share from that word. What and how a reader experiences meditation upon the text is unique to each person and to each passage of scripture.

Once the reader has experienced the emergence of the Word from the text and has paused to allow the Word to speak in some way, he or she is ready for the third movement of *Lectio*, which is *prayer*. This step is much like Wesley's instructions to allow the biblical text to search one's heart and to comfort, convict, challenge, or instruct the reader in the way of holiness. The reader begins to pray with whatever was revealed from the text during meditation.

The ongoing commitment to live what's been revealed, as a response to God's love and grace, is the fourth movement of *Lectio*, which is *contemplation*. This process is also consistent with Wesley's instructions to immediately put into practice whatever is given to us as we read the Bible. Contemplation means that I will consciously think and pray along these lines, look for the opportunity that will surely arise, and act upon that opportunity with God's help.

LOOKING AHEAD AND CLOSING PRAYER (5 Minutes)

Have the class share joys and prayer concerns, and invite them to be in prayer for each other over the coming week. Invite someone to close in prayer or read a few verses from Psalm 119.

Session 4

Three: The Lord's Supper

INTRODUCTION

Two of the most visible means of grace for Methodists and Wesleyans are *sacraments*: the Lord's Supper and baptism. "Sacraments are special means of grace that are 'outward signs of inwardly received grace.'" The meaning of the Lord's Supper is closely linked to the meaning of baptism. The Lord's Supper is a way to remember what happened at baptism. When we participate in the Lord's Supper, we confess and renounce our sin, state our intent to follow Jesus, and commit ourselves to live in union with Christ and his mission.

This session will help your class

1. recognize why participating in the Lord's Supper is indispensable for experiencing God's love;

2. identify the barriers that prevent us from experiencing the blessings of God's love; and

3. experience the Lord's Supper.

GATHERING (5 Minutes)

Invite participants to read in unison the lyrics from the Charles Wesley hymn "O Thou Who This Mysterious Bread" (*The United Methodist Hymnal*, no. 613).

O Thou who this mysterious bread didst in Emmaus break,
return, herewith our souls to feed,
    and to thy followers speak.
Unseal the volume of thy grace,
    apply the gospel word;
open our eyes to see they face,
    our hearts to know the Lord.

Invite participants to reflect silently on those words for a minute. After the silence, have them turn to a person next to them to share what words, phrases, or ideas resonate with them.

Ask a participant to open the session with a word of prayer.

REFLECTIONS ON THE READING (10 Minutes)

The author introduces us to Henri Nouwen's image about Holy Communion. Read aloud: "We are taken, blessed, broken and given. We are gathered into community, something like a multigrain loaf. God kneads us into one loaf and then blesses us, forgiving us of our sins and setting us on a path of healing and reconciliation. At the benediction God 'breaks' the loaf of our community into many pieces by sending us forth to embody Jesus in the world. As communities of faith we become the Communion bread that God gives to the world."

Invite the class to break up into two or three groups, and have each group reflect together on one of the following statements in this chapter:

- "We are taken, blessed, broken, and given" (p. 17).

- "The real meaning of Christianity is to feed the hungry, both spiritually and literally" (p. 19).

- "The sacrament of the Lord's Supper [is the way] to receive the blessings that God offers" (p. 21).

Ask each group to describe the meaning of these statements, perhaps restating the meaning in their own words or explaining how the statement describes a means for grace. Then have each group share their explanations with the other.

When all the groups have shared, ask the whole class to reflect together on the following questions:

1. What are the obstacles that often prevent us from experiencing the blessings of the Lord's Supper?

2. What can we do to overcome these obstacles?

VIDEO SEGMENT (15 Minutes)

Video segment featuring Elaine A. Heath, author of *Five Means of Grace*, in conversation with theology professor Joerg Rieger.

VIDEO DISCUSSION QUESTIONS (10 Minutes)

1. Elaine describes how the household dinner table has become an expression of the Lord's Supper. How is this understanding of Communion similar to or different from your understanding and experience of Communion?

2. What is the meaning of the open Table in United Methodist Communion practice?

3. Has Communion ever been a healing experience (emotionally, spiritually, or physically) for you or someone you know? Is there a connection between

our healing and becoming God's "one loaf" gift of love for others (see Isa 58:8)?

PRACTICAL APPLICATION (10 Minutes)

As the meeting comes to a close, review together the Communion liturgy and baptismal vows that are in the *United Methodist Hymnal*. Offer a prayer of commitment that draws language from either or both of these liturgies. You may wish to use a symbolic action such as making the sign of the cross on one another's hands with water or, if possible, participate in the Lord's Supper with each other.

LOOKING AHEAD AND CLOSING PRAYER (5 Minutes)

Have the class share joys and prayer concerns, and invite them to be in prayer for each other over the coming week. Invite someone to close in prayer.

Four: Fasting

INTRODUCTION

Abundance can be a blessing. We give thanks for abundant friends, family, health, and food. And for that reason, fasting is probably the most challenging practice for Protestant Christians, most of whom rarely miss a meal.

As a means of grace, fasting is based in denial. Fasting is a *no*. When Christians fast as a spiritual practice, we accept the denial of a relentless need in the body, mind, or spirit. Yet fasting also reminds us that our needs can be selfish and addictive. In the midst of distraction by gluttony, it is difficult to experience God's love for others. It can also make it more difficult to love oneself.

This session will help your class

1. learn how deep intercessory fasting can channel God's grace for others who suffer;

2. reflect on the spiritual and physical reasons for fasting; and

3. recognize that fasting prepares the body, mind, and spirit for carrying out God's mission.

GATHERING (5 Minutes)

Invite participants to reflect on the following image in the opening paragraph of the chapter, taken from John Wesley's sermon "Means of Grace" in which he says that fasting without a properly motivated heart is only a "poor, dead, empty thing: separate from God, it is a dry leaf, a shadow." Describe ways in which you have experienced religious practices or rituals that felt like "dry leaves" or "shadows."

Focus on the analogy to a dry leaf. Ask for a participant to share about the benefits from a fasting experience.

Ask another participant to open the session with a word of prayer.

REFLECTIONS ON THE READING (10 Minutes)

For Jesus in Luke 4:1-13, immediately after he is baptized and as he prepares to begin ministry, Jesus is *driven* by the Spirit into the wilderness. Ask for a participant to reflect on a time when she or he was "driven" through a wilderness experience. What did it feel like? Empty? Lonely? Was a difficult decision the reason for the wilderness? Did the desert experience offer clarity about a purpose or the future?

Some Christian traditions include fasting as a regular weekly practice. Greek Orthodox Christians practice fasting on Wednesday and Fridays. John Wesley adopted this practice too.

Ask participants to reflect on the following statements from the chapter:

- "Despite all the ways we normally behave as if we are in control, we are not" (p. 44).

- "As we bring into prayer the suffering of those for whom we fast, we simultaneously feel our own weakness" (p. 44).

- "Fasting returns us to our deep dependence upon God" (p. 44).

VIDEO SEGMENT (15 Minutes)

Video segment featuring Elaine A. Heath, author of *Five Means of Grace*, in conversation with theology professor Joerg Rieger.

VIDEO DISCUSSION QUESTIONS (15 Minutes)

1. As you read this chapter about fasting or watched the video conversation, what did you learn that was new? What challenged you?

2. In this session, fasting is linked with intercessory prayer, illustrated with the Gospel story about the boy whom the disciples couldn't help even though they had a measure of faith. When, if ever, have you encountered a situation that required deep intercessory prayer that included fasting, and then saw a breakthrough?

3. Elaine says, "Fasting brings us into solidarity with other people who are suffering, and that changes us." How can fasting be both a channel for grace in your own life and a way to share grace with others?

4. What is the difference between compassion, advocacy, and solidarity?

PRACTICAL APPLICATION (5 Minutes)

In your group, decide on a common fast of some kind that you can practice for the coming week. When your group meets next week for its final session, discuss how you experienced the fast.

LOOKING AHEAD AND CLOSING PRAYER (5 Minutes)

Have the class share joys and prayer concerns, and invite them to be in prayer for each other over the coming week. Invite someone to close in prayer.

Five: Christian Conferencing

INTRODUCTION

Millions of people have left the church, meaning they no longer participate in weekend worship or other discipleship experiences, since the 1960s. Many causes for this attrition are suggested, such as relevance to daily life, boring worship, or judgmental and legalistic leaders. The causes are as complex as each individual, but a large group of "de-churched" persons still identify as Christian or evangelical, even as they (and observers of the culture) prefer to say they are "spiritual but not religious." By this they express disappointment in organized religion.

This session will help your class

1. learn why regular Christian conferencing (meaning worship and discipleship) is an indispensable means of grace;

2. discover that there are alternative fresh expressions for Christian conferencing in nontraditional settings; and

3. learn the three essential elements for any group experiencing the means of grace through Christian conferencing.

GATHERING (5 Minutes)

In this chapter, the author describes the most basic meaning of church, or *ekklesia*. How does this meaning compare to your experience of church?

Invite participants to reflect on why they do or don't participate in worship. Ask for a participant to describe a worship service or small-group experience that stirred the person's heart so much that he or she was transformed and changed a behavior or pursued a new place of service toward others.

Have the class share joys and prayer concerns, and invite them to be in prayer for each other. By doing this each week (this time at the beginning of the last session for this study), remind participants that this sharing is one of the ways to experience the means of grace through the experience of Christian conferencing. Invite someone to open the session in prayer.

REFLECTIONS ON THE READING (15 Minutes)

Have participants turn to a neighbor and share recollections of a family member or friend who guided them into weekend worship or small-group experiences through a church. As part of their reflection, invite participants to think of reasons it might be difficult for them to participate in worship or in church with regularity.

Have the class work on completing the following sentences based on the prior four means of grace:

- "We pray to God so that _____."
- "We eat the Lord's Supper so that _____."
- "We search the Scriptures so that _____."
- "We fast so that _____."

For each sentence completion, have the group brainstorm ways that each means of grace contributes to a tangible way of serving others. In other words, how does each of these means of experiencing God's grace relate to the impact God can make through us on the lives of others?

This chapter articulates three essential elements for experiencing the means of grace through Christian conferencing (p. 56). Read these elements aloud and ask the participants to comment on where they think these elements are present in their lives:

1. The group is gathered in the name of Jesus, as described with regard to Matthew 18:20 ("where two or three are gathered").

2. The practices of the group foster deep spiritual friendships that lead to growth in personal and corporate holiness and genuine community.

3. The group is engaged in missional ministry beyond itself, thus it is *kenotic* (which means "self giving").

VIDEO SEGMENT (15 Minutes)

Video segment featuring Elaine A. Heath, author of *Five Means of Grace*, in conversation with theology professor Joerg Rieger.

VIDEO DISCUSSION QUESTIONS (10 Minutes)

1. Have you practiced Christian conferencing in a way that changed your life? What happened? What changed?

2. What's the difference between many of our small groups and Sunday school classes (casual spiritual

friendship experiences) and what Wesley meant by Christian conferencing?

3. What are the God reasons for being part of a diverse community with different kinds of people? (Hint: iron sharpens iron, one body with different parts, not political correctness but rather God's imagination about who we are made to be)

To build upon ideas from participants, consider as your next group experience the Bible study resource *Fresh Expressions: A New Kind of Methodist Church for People Not in Church* by Kenneth H. Carter Jr. and Audrey Warren (ISBN 9781501849206).

PRACTICAL APPLICATION (5 Minutes)

Following a rule of life is core to Methodist DNA, yet very few Methodists today intentionally do so. Why do you think this is the case?

As you consider following a Methodist rule of life, consider the General Rules (summarized in Rueben P. Job's *Three Simple Rules*) or a modern adaptation, such as the use of United Methodist membership vows—to faithfully participate in our ministries by our prayers, our presence, our gifts, our service, and our witness. What would be the most challenging aspect for you? What would come easily?

CLOSING PRAYER AND CLOSING THIS STUDY (5 Minutes)

As your group concludes this study, discuss ways that your church could more intentionally teach and practice the ordinary means of grace as presented in this book. Offer a closing prayer for your church in response to whatever surfaces during your conversation.

The Means of Grace Are Spiritual Practices

"The thing is," my neighbor said conspiratorially, "I really love to iron. I iron everything. I iron every day." Corrine, a Lutheran, lived across the street and was a faithful member of a neighborhood spiritual formation group that I led. She had grown up in the Depression, kept a very tidy house, and was a fabulous cook. She adored Elvis Presley. I adored her.

"What is it about ironing that you find so meaningful?" I laughed.

"When I iron, it's a kind of ritual. I put the water in the iron and plug it in. As I press the fabric, the steam rises, all fragrant and clean. All the wrinkles go away. One by one they go away. Something about the steam, the wrinkles, and the regular movement of the iron across the board brings peace to me. I feel at home and at ease. Things that were troubling me don't seem so overwhelming. I even feel closer to God. It's a spiritual thing." She paused, then grinned sheepishly. "You probably think I'm crazy," she said.

"No, Corrine, I think you are a contemplative," I answered. "You have found in ironing what others have found through forms of prayer that involve the five senses, bodily movement, and a repetitive activity that quiets the mind and opens the heart to God's presence."

"Golly," she said. "Who knew?"

What Corrine discovered in ironing is a "means of grace," to use John Wesley's language. That is, ironing is a pathway for her to encounter the healing, peaceful, loving presence of God. Thomas Keating might note that, for Corrine, ironing became a form of centering prayer, a way to descend from her mind into her heart. Wesley didn't write about ironing as a means of grace, but he would likely affirm Corrine's experience, especially since Corrine regularly participated in worship, partook of the Lord's Supper, read the Bible, prayed, and took part in our neighborhood spiritual formation group. Wesley felt that anything and everything can become a channel of God's love for those who are always open to and seeking God.[1]

With wonderful generosity Wesley argues that people can experience God without external acts such as reading the Bible or fasting. The acts themselves are simply channels through which grace flows. He also firmly denounces empty ritualism in which Christians go through the motions of prayer, worship, and so on but have no desire for God's transforming work in their lives. Indeed some of his harshest words in sermons and elsewhere are directed toward Christians who love "a form of godliness without the power."[2]

But Wesley was concerned about these spiritual disciplines because he faced in his own context a "spiritual but not religious" movement of Christians who left the church and abandoned the means of grace. These Christians felt it was no longer necessary to read the Bible, partake of the Lord's Supper, gather in worship, or engage in other ordinary Christian spiritual disciplines because Christ's direct love was enough. Wesley was alarmed about the corrosive effect that this movement would have upon Christian commitment, because most of us need habitual practices that daily open our hearts and minds to God's transforming love. Moreover, without regular reminders we will drift away from God's missional call to love and serve our neighbors. In all things Wesley's goal is for Christians to participate in God's good work, carrying the love and power of Jesus into the world. He calls this process of increasing holiness "going on to perfection."

This book guides readers through the five means of grace that John Wesley called "instituted," meaning these are spiritual practices that were instituted in the New Testament and are binding for all time and in all places. The five means of grace are prayer, searching the Scriptures, the Lord's Supper, fasting, and Christian conferencing.

One beautiful aspect of Wesley's theology is that spiritual practices are seamlessly integrated with practices of loving our neighbors well. This is why Wesley said there is no holiness but social holiness. A life of genuine prayer inevitably leads to a life of hospitality, mercy, and justice. Through this book we will consider how each of the five means of grace help us as communities of faith to pray more deeply and live more missionally as followers of Jesus Christ.

1

Prayer

We were sitting in Betty's office debriefing after I led a meeting of the women's discipleship group that Betty, an associate pastor at our large Pentecostal church, had started years ago. Her staff responsibilities included disciple formation and pastoral care. Betty had over many months coaxed me into joining the group a couple of years before that, telling me it was a gathering "by invitation only, for special ladies," which sounded mysterious but I was pretty sure meant "for Christians who are slow learners."

When I finally went to the nameless group I realized with dawning joy that the dozen or so women were a ragtag group of disciples who wanted to learn to pray deeply and to hear God speaking to them through the Bible. Like me, some of them had experienced significant trauma in their lives, so they couldn't be satisfied with pat answers to tough questions such as "Why does a good God allow children to suffer abuse?" With great patience and wisdom, Betty taught and mentored all of us.

After a couple of years of attending this group, Betty asked me to take over leadership of the group. This was all part of her careful mentoring process to help me awaken to God's call. I felt overwhelmed by the task, but Betty was insistent that I should do it, so I agreed. Within a few months of taking over, the group's membership had expanded to several dozen women, most of whom were not from our church and many of whom were new to Christianity. I was doing my best to help them know what it meant to follow Jesus even though I was very much a beginner myself.

So it was that on this day Betty said to me, "When you guide new Christians in following Jesus, don't start with doctrine. If you do, you will ruin them. Instead, start with prayer. Teach them to gaze into the face of Jesus, who gazes back with infinite love." I looked at her and saw Jesus gazing at me with infinite love. I loved Betty, but inwardly I balked because I was certain that teaching doctrine was more important than "gazing" prayer, whatever that was. Betty went on to say that people who learn this way of praying develop the ability to tell the difference between doctrine that honors Jesus and doctrine that leads to legalism, quarrels, and strife.

It took another decade of living and some experiences of suffering before I truly understood the wisdom Betty offered me that day. "Gazing into the face of Jesus who gazes back with infinite love" is a contemplative practice that grounds us in a beloved relationship with God. We are already dearly loved by God. We can't diminish or lose God's love for us. It's this crucial awareness of being loved that increasingly enables us to let down our guard with God and to become like Adam and Eve before the fall, "naked and unashamed" before God. From an experience of vulnerability, trust, honesty, and safety, we are able to grow in holiness. We are able to let go of sinful, self-defeating, destructive thoughts and behaviors. We increasingly find ourselves demonstrating the same hospitable love toward others that God demonstrates toward us. We do indeed become able to determine whether a doctrine is consistent with the love of God revealed in Christ. We are enabled to live as Christ in the world.

The Christian faith is all about a relationship of love, trust, and vulnerability, on God's part and on ours. Prayer is the essence of that relationship. It is more than speaking and listening, more than liturgy or silence. Prayer is the very breath of God, breathing life into us, opening us to who God is, to who we are, and to this world that God loves. The breath of God brings life, healing, renewal, comfort, challenge, and direction. Just as breathing is necessary for life in our physical bodies, prayer is necessary for spiritual life.

There are many meaningful forms of prayer—including worship, intercession, thanksgiving, and lament—but fundamentally prayer is a practice of being present to God, who is always present to us.[1] Or in Betty's words, it is gazing into the face of Jesus, who gazes back with infinite love.

Whatever forms we use, prayer is meant to open ourselves to God's love and presence, God's character, and God's activity in the world, which increasingly leads us to participate in God's life in the world. Because prayer connects us to who God is and what God is doing, all the ordinary means of grace, as John Wesley named them, are expressions of prayer, for all of them are intended to draw us close to God in loving relationship. As you read each chapter in this book, notice how each means of grace is a type of prayer, opening us to God.

Now that we understand prayer as being present to God who is present to us, let's turn our attention to ways of praying that are common within various streams of Methodism.[2]

One of the common ways that Methodists pray is the use of a daily office, or set times of prayer every day, using a liturgical resource. The use of a daily office was central to John and Charles Wesley's Anglican spirituality. In fact, the *Book of Common Prayer* was John Wesley's favorite book, second only to the Bible.

The United Methodist Hymnal includes Orders of Daily Praise and Prayer, brief liturgies that can be used in the morning and evening, especially in a gathering. Since Methodism emerged from the Anglican Church, the form of the prayers is similar to prayers found in the *Book of Common Prayer*. Scripture readings in these daily liturgies are typically referenced to the Revised Common Lectionary, a system of reading the Bible that enables readers to work through most of the Bible over a three-year cycle, while paying attention to the seasons of the church year such as Lent and Advent.

For persons who aren't from liturgical traditions, the use of a prayer book or liturgies can seem confining or impersonal. However, when used consistently and in an informed way, over time these structured prayers can help Christians attend to God more deeply as well as more broadly. Especially during times of stress or when it is difficult to pray, these liturgies help Christians join with others around the world who also pray this way. Some well-loved devotional books in the Wesleyan traditions that use a liturgical approach include *This Day: A Wesleyan Way of Prayer* (Abingdon, 2004), and the original *A Guide to Prayer for Ministers and Other Servants* (The Upper Room, 1998) along with subsequent volumes. *The Upper Room* is a very popular and simple guide to daily prayer that is published quarterly and used by millions of people around the world.

The value of using orders for morning and evening prayer really came home to me many years ago while a colleague and I led a group of students on a pilgrimage to Iona, Scotland, and Northumberland, England. The goal of the pilgrimage was to become familiar with ancient and contemporary Celtic Christian spirituality and missional practice. While on Iona we attended morning and evening prayer at the Iona Abbey, where the liturgy was from the Iona Community. After several days one of the students exclaimed, "I just love going to morning and evening prayer. This is all new to me." When I asked what he especially liked he said, "For one thing there is no sermon." Of course, we all laughed since every student present had to take a preaching class, and most of them were headed for pastoral ministry! When I asked why the absence of a sermon felt life-giving, many students replied that because the worship was focused on prayer rather than the work of delivering or listening to a sermon, they were able to more quickly "descend from the mind into the heart" in their worship. The structure for the prayer guided them uniquely into deepened experiences of God's love for themselves and for the world. They also found the themes for each day helpful in focusing their prayers toward the needs of the whole world, rather than just their own locale.

Another source of prayer for which Methodists are well known is the hymnal. Charles Wesley penned more than nine thousand hymns during his lifetime, though only a small portion of them are still sung. Hymnody is one key to teaching theology to congregations, and has been since the beginning of Methodism. To put it simply, we sing what we believe, just as we pray what we believe. Many of the hymns in *The United Methodist Hymnal* are prayers set to music. For example, "Maker, in Whom We Live" by Charles Wesley is a song of love and commitment addressed directly to each member of the Trinity. Verse one sets the tone:

> Maker, in whom we live, in whom we are and move,
> the glory, power, and praise receive for thy creating love.
> Let all the angel throng give thanks to God on high,
> while earth repeats the joyful song and echoes to the sky.[3]

While the use of a daily office, the *Book of Common Prayer*, and hymnody are core practices in Methodist spirituality, John Wesley also used extemporaneous prayer, or unscripted prayer. In a journal entry dated August 4, 1788, in which he defends his lifelong commitment to the Anglican Church and its doctrine, Wesley states that despite never straying from Anglican doctrine he did at times transgress standard liturgical practices and use extemporaneous prayer—but only because the ministry context demanded it.[4]

Extemporaneous prayer can be anxiety-provoking for persons formed in a strongly liturgical tradition. I've met many lifelong Methodists who felt unable to pray aloud unless reading a printed prayer from an official resource. The thought of praying the wrong words or making a grammatical error was paralyzing, thus they couldn't bring themselves to spontaneously offer a simple table grace, make a hospital visit to pray aloud for a sick friend, or offer a compassionate prayer for a friend going through a hard time. Their spiritual formation had led them to believe that prayer is mostly a formal speech that we make to God, who in his divine majesty requires correct grammar and theology and impressive delivery. Because of this unfortunate misconception, these dear Christians were missing out on the profound gift of simple prayer that arises from silence within and gives voice to what emerges. Extemporaneous prayer can be a prayer of worship, thanksgiving, petition, penitence, complaint, or all of the above and more. This kind of prayer is organic in that it is deeply contextualized to the situation and reflects the personality and spirituality of the persons praying. Within John Wesley's lifetime Methodists came to be known broadly as persons who used extemporaneous prayer along with formal, liturgical prayer.

When I taught evangelism to seminary students, a new friend, Sherry, offered to pray for me on a regular basis. Usually she prayed in silence interrupted only by occasional words. One day when she came to pray, I told her that several students wanted to learn how to live in intentional community and to practice hospitality and engage in the concerns of the neighborhood. The problem, I said, was that I didn't have funds for a house where the students could experience this kind of life as part of their education, yet I felt God calling me to find a house and guide these students. Sherry nodded her head and began to pray in silence as usual. After a while she quietly said, "The house is coming. I see it." Two weeks later a neighbor who knew nothing about my students or their vocations, and very little about me, called me out of the blue and offered a rental house at no cost other than utilities if I "had some students who would live there and take care of the place." The house was in the kind of neighborhood where the students hoped to live—multicultural, mixed income, and close to public transportation. Sherry's extemporaneous and intercessory prayer was the means through which grace flowed to supply a specific resource for a God-breathed ministry.

While prayer is the first of the five means of grace, every means of grace is a form of prayer because each is a pathway for Christians to know and do God's will. In the next chapter we focus on Wesley's practice of "searching the Scriptures," a form of prayer in which God speaks to us through the Bible.

2
Searching the Scriptures

We rode along in the 1976 Ford pickup making small talk, eating wheat crackers, and trying not to cry. The daily trip was two hours to the hospital in Springfield, Missouri, where my father was critically ill. This day it was my turn to drive. Throughout my childhood, both parents were hostile toward the church, having had unpleasant encounters with religious folk. Nonetheless, in their late sixties Jesus won them over. They were both new Christians when I got the call that Dad was sick. Within hours I was on my way.

Mom needed help with Dad in the hospital, and there was work that had to be done around their small farm. As we talked about the challenges that would face them if Dad survived, we got onto the subject of God's help in times of need. I was driving, and Mom was in the passenger seat. Mom asked if there was a passage of scripture that could help. I was still a beginner myself, having just started leading "the group for special ladies." I pointed to the Bible in my tote bag. It was huge, a black, leather-bound Thompson Chain-Reference New International Version with an impressive zippered case. "You can look up words like *comfort* and *help* in the back," I said. "We'll find something." All of a sudden Mom looked at me, stricken, the Bible in one hand, her cigarette in the other. "Do you reckon God minds if I smoke while I read the Bible?" she asked. She was serious.

In John Wesley's terms, Mom wanted to "search the Scriptures," one of the means of grace. We hoped that God might provide guidance and comfort at a time of great uncertainty. In her simple question, Mom raised powerful theological issues: What are the conditions under which a person can "search the Scriptures" and encounter therein the living God? What might be obstacles to seeing and hearing God through scripture when we do read the Bible? How does one go about reading the Bible so that scriptures come to mind helpfully when we need them?

The term "searching the Scriptures" is old-fashioned, as if we are looking for buried treasure. Yet this is an accurate description for a truly Wesleyan way to read the Bible. In his preface to the *Explanatory Notes upon the New Testament*, one of his most important texts, John Wesley describes his purpose in having done the background research and then having written the commentary notes. The *Explanatory Notes* are not written for intellectuals or professional scholars. Rather, they are written "for plain, unlettered men, who understand only their mother tongue, and yet reverence and love the word of God, and have a desire to save their souls."[1] This comment, along with many other statements Wesley makes about the Bible, demonstrates that for Wesley, reading the Bible is for the explicit purpose of Christian transformation. We "search" the Scriptures, leaving no stone unturned, expecting to encounter the living God and discover life-changing guidance in its pages.

John Wesley was sometimes mocked for his deep love of Scripture. Some of his detractors called him a "Bible moth." He called himself a "man of one book," an interesting designation considering he read widely from many disciplines, including science and medicine. The most popular book in his lifetime that he wrote was *Primitive Physic*, a guide to holistic medicine. When he referenced himself as a man of one book, then, what he was referring to was the central role the Bible played in his thought and life. In reading through his journals, sermons, and other writing it is obvious that his very cadences of speech have been shaped by the Bible.

Even so, Wesley didn't understand the Bible to be infallible in the way some interpreters prefer today. The Anglican Articles of Faith and the Confession that guided Wesley's doctrine of Scripture never refer to the text of Scripture as "inspired," nor do they call the Bible "the Word of God." It's clear that Wesley believed the Bible was inspired by God, but Randy Maddox points out that "it is doubtful that he should be characterized as an inerrantist in the contemporary sense of the term."[2] The Confession states that the Bible "reveals the word of God."[3] Despite his deep love of Scripture, Wesley never preached a sermon focusing exclusively on the Bible, nor did he write a treatise about it. Scripture rather was the water in which he swam, as it permeated his thought, words, and actions.

In his preface to the *Explanatory Notes upon the Old Testament*, Wesley advises the following. First, the reader should set aside time morning and evening, habitually, to read a full chapter each from both the Old and New Testaments. If there is not time for two chapters, the reader should select one chapter or a portion of one chapter. The goal in this reading is for one purpose: *to know and do the will of God*. Because the goal is Christian formation, Wesley urges readers to keep in mind at all times the basic themes and doctrines of the Christian faith as interpretive lenses. The reader must pray for the Holy Spirit to illumine his or her mind to receive the spiritual understanding of the text, something that doesn't happen automatically and without which the reading will be useless. While reading one should move slowly through the passage, pausing to reflect often so that the text can aid the reader in self-examination, with the scripture sometimes comforting, sometimes challenging, and sometimes convicting the reader of the need for change. Finally, one should immediately put into practice any guidance or instructions that come through this twice-daily practice of searching the Scriptures.[4]

These instructions, emerging from Wesley's own discipline of searching the Scriptures, have much in common with the ancient method of praying with Scripture, called *Lectio Divina*, or "sacred reading."[5] The practice of *Lectio* began before the sixth century, originating in the Benedictine-Cistercian traditions. It is a prayer based on a scripture that is accessible to almost anyone, and it seems that this method may have influenced Wesley's structure for searching the Scriptures, though he doesn't use the phrase *Lectio Divina*.

Lectio Divina has four movements, which don't always follow in the sequence set forth below. The reading is done with an orientation toward listening to the Holy Spirit, who may speak through the text. This principle is in keeping with the Confession that guided Wesley, that the Bible reveals the word of God. To prepare for reading one should quiet oneself and open one's heart to the Holy Spirit in readiness for whatever may be given. The intention is to hear whatever the Holy Spirit may say through the text and to pray with it and then live into it in whatever ways God asks.

Reading is the first movement. A short passage of scripture, no longer than one chapter and preferably just one story or short section, is read through slowly, at least twice. As the reader moves slowly in a listening manner through the text, he or she may sense a phrase, word, sentence, or concept emerging from the text, drawing the reader's attention. At that point the reader should pause. As Wesley instructs in his preface to the *Explanatory Notes upon the Old Testament*, the pause allows the text to examine the reader.

This pause is the second movement of *Lectio*: meditation. In this part, the reader reflects on the word, image, or phrase that surfaced from the reading. It is time for a deeper listening to what God wants to share from that word. What and how a reader experiences meditation upon the text is unique to each person and to each passage of scripture.

In teaching *Lectio Divina* to congregations when I was a pastor, I liked to use John 4, the story of the woman at the well. People experienced the story in different ways, some more intellectually, some more emotionally as they entered into the narrative of Jesus talking to an outcast Samaritan woman and drinking from her cup. The meditation upon the text was unique to each person, according to his or her own journey and way of engaging the text.

Once the reader has experienced the emergence of the Word from the text and has paused to allow the Word to speak in some way, he or she is ready for the third movement of *Lectio*, which is prayer. This step is much like Wesley's instructions to allow the biblical text to search one's heart and to comfort, convict, challenge, or instruct the reader in the way of holiness. The reader begins to pray with whatever was revealed from the text during meditation. For example, if the story in John 4 calls forth an awareness that I've been judgmental of an outcast in my community, perhaps my prayer will focus on blessing that person and asking God for an opportunity to get to know that person as someone God loves.

The ongoing commitment to live what's been revealed, as a response to God's love and grace, is the fourth movement of *Lectio*, which is contemplation. This process is also consistent with Wesley's instructions to immediately put into practice whatever is given to us as we read the Bible. Returning again to the example from John 4, after praying for the outcast person in my community and asking God for an opportunity to get to know the person, contemplation means that I will consciously think and pray along these lines, look for the opportunity that will surely arise, and act upon that opportunity with God's help.

The goal in searching the Scriptures is to increasingly bear the love and grace of God to our neighbors because God's word has become alive in us. Sometimes when searching the Scriptures, we don't seem to notice anything that speaks to us. We may not feel anything or find ourselves drawn to an image or idea in the text. There are times when we read the Bible and, despite our best intentions, it seems dry to us. At such times we may rest in the love of God and simply let the experience be what it is. The important thing is to regularly pray with Scripture in this way. Over time, as we habitually search the Scriptures with our hearts open to God, we will be, in the words of Robert Mulholland, "shaped by the word."[6]

Riding along in the truck that day, neither Mom nor I knew what the future would bring. She did find a passage using my briefcase-sized Bible and read it aloud so that we could both hear it. We talked about God as our ever-present help in times of need. Dad did recover to live a few more years. My mother became an avid student of the Bible and a strong woman of prayer. When she died at age ninety-six, she was known far and wide as a woman of deep faith who helped many other people put their trust in God. She even finally gave up cigarettes, with

God's help. She told everyone she just couldn't justify the expense any longer, but I know for a fact that God spoke to her through Psalm 139, her favorite psalm. Searching the Scriptures led her to the knowledge that in God's view she was "fearfully and wonderfully made," so she might take better care of her lungs.

3

The Lord's Supper

We gather in the kitchen where a feast is spread across the counter—warm, homemade bread and jam from residents of the Bruderhof house,[1] vegetables from the Community Supported Agriculture (CSA) farm next door, meatloaf from friends who live in another community house a few miles away. And for a special treat, homemade ice cream and cookies. There are usually at least a dozen of us, sometimes twice that many. Tonight we gather at Spring Forest, the intentional community where I live in Hillsborough, North Carolina, to share a meal and pray with others who live in or are interested in intentional communities in the area.[2] We gather as a loose network of communities once a month but stay in touch in various ways between times, helping each other with life and ministries such as refugee resettlement.

As we eat the bread and raise a toast we remember that this is how the Lord's Supper took place in the early church. The bread and wine were part of a real supper, with diverse guests from different houses gathered under one roof. Members of my community, Spring Forest, love the liturgical tradition of Holy Communion, of which we partake monthly at the United Methodist congregation where we worship. Nonetheless, we experience our own dinner table as an expression of the Lord's Supper too. Grace is given to us through sharing food and drink. Christ speaks to us as we talk about how we encounter God in our work, our lives, and our spiritual journeys in recent days. We strategize and pray about ministry matters in our various houses. We feel the longing of God's heart as we discuss and pray about current events in our nation and world. Closing the evening in benediction, we remember that we are called into fellowship as the body of Christ in order to be given as bread and wine to our neighbors. Our monthly experience of "dinner church" doesn't preclude belonging to and participating in established congregations, nor does it negate our appreciation for the sacraments administered in traditional ways. It does, however, bring home to us with clarity the missional meaning of the Lord's Supper. We take Christ's life into ourselves so that we can bear Christ's life among our neighbors.

The Lord's Supper is one of two sacraments in Methodist traditions, the other being baptism. Sacraments are special means of grace that are an "outward sign of inward grace."[3] When we are baptized we "renounce the spiritual forces of wickedness [and] reject the evil powers of this world." We accept our call to "resist evil, injustice, and oppression in whatever forms they present themselves." We commit ourselves to Jesus Christ "in union with the church which Christ has opened to people of all ages, nations, and races."[4] Baptism is the ritual that marks our entry into a life of Christian discipleship. Long after our own baptism, each time we witness the baptism of others, we renew our own commitment to Christ through the words of the baptismal liturgy.

The meaning of the Lord's Supper is closely linked to the meaning of baptism. The connection becomes obvious when we look at the Communion liturgy. Each time we partake of the Lord's Supper we confess and renounce our sin, state our intent to follow Jesus, and commit ourselves to live in union with Christ and his mission. During the epiclesis (or the invocation of the Holy Spirit) we pray:

> Pour out your Holy Spirit on us gathered here, and on these gifts of bread and wine. Make them be for us the body and blood of Christ, that we may be for the world the body of Christ, redeemed by his blood. By your Spirit make us one with Christ, one with each other, and one in ministry to all the world, until Christ comes in final victory, and we feast at his heavenly banquet.[5]

In his beautiful meditation *Life of the Beloved*, Henri J. M. Nouwen draws from the metaphor of the bread and wine of the Lord's Supper to describe four movements in the Christian life.[6] We are taken, blessed, broken, and given. We are gathered into community, something like a multigrain loaf. God kneads us into one loaf and then blesses us, forgiving us of our sins and setting us on a path of healing and reconciliation. At the benediction God "breaks" the loaf of our community into many pieces by sending us forth to embody Jesus in the world. As communities of faith, we become the Communion bread that God gives to the world.

The Scriptures show us that God loves us dearly (see 1 John 3:1). Just as God spoke to Jesus at his baptism, God speaks to us today: *You are my dearly loved child. In you I am well pleased.* God's love binds us to God forever. In the embodied prayer of Holy Communion we remember, we celebrate, and we commit ourselves to full participation in the mission of God.

John Wesley believed that Christians should partake of the Lord's Supper as often as possible. In his sermon "The Duty of Constant Communion," Wesley argues that sharing at the Lord's Table enables us to leave our sins behind and live as holy people. He makes a strong argument that daily Communion was the way of the early church and thus should be the pattern of contemporary Christians. Most of the sermon is a rebuttal of the usual excuses Wesley's contemporaries gave for avoiding Communion.

To prepare for the Lord's Supper, he teaches, Christians should truly wish to follow the commandments of God and to receive all the promises of God. One of the notable aspects of Methodist faith and practice is the "open table" or the practice of inviting any and all who wish to partake. The liturgy issues this invitation: "Christ our Lord invites to his table all who love him, who earnestly repent of their sin and seek to live in peace with one another."[7] Wesley believed that even if persons didn't know Christ, they could come to know Christ's salvation in the act of Holy Communion if their hearts longed to know him and they came to the Table with that hunger.

In her memoir, *Take This Bread: A Radical Conversion,* Sara Miles tells the story of her extremely unlikely conversion while walking unexpectedly into St. Gregory of Nyssa Episcopal Church and to the

Communion Table.[8] Miles, a cynical forty-six-year-old war correspondent, experienced exactly what Methodists believe the Lord's Supper can do when the Table is open to all. The Lord's Supper became the means of grace that welcomed Miles into the Christian faith and revealed her new vocation to her. At the Table Miles underwent a Damascus Road[9] experience in which God showed her that the real meaning of Christianity is to feed the hungry, both spiritually and literally.

The Lord's Supper is a potent, embodied prayer through which we align ourselves fully with God's work of making all things new. Each time we eat the bread and drink the cup we say yes to all that Christ is and all that he invites us to be, together. One of the earliest hymns of the church focuses on the union of the church with Christ in his way of being in the world:

Adopt the attitude that was in Christ Jesus:

Though he was in the form of God,
    he did not consider being equal with God something to exploit.
But he emptied himself
    by taking the form of a slave
    and by becoming like human beings.
    When he found himself in the form of a human,
    he humbled himself by becoming obedient to the point of death,
    even death on a cross.
Therefore, God highly honored him
    and gave him a name above all names,
    so that at the name of Jesus everyone
    in heaven, on earth, and under the earth might bow
    and every tongue confess that
    Jesus Christ is Lord, to the glory of God the Father. (Phil 2:5-11 CEB)

The Greek word for "emptied himself" is *kenosis*. It means to give oneself to others. This hymn is one of the most important passages of scripture for the church today, calling the church to repent of the ways in which we have not loved our neighbors and have not taken the role of servant among our neighbors. Too often our posture toward those who are not in the church is one of censure, judgment, or animosity. We do not see such attitudes or behaviors in Jesus in the Gospel narratives. The reason that we bend our knees and confess that Jesus Christ is Lord is not that Jesus and his followers will take the world with violence or will shame and terrify the world into submission. Rather, the world comes to trust in Jesus's love when it experiences the church living in the way of Jesus, the way of *kenosis*. Participating in the Lord's Supper can help us do that.

Charles Wesley's Communion hymn "O Thou Who This Mysterious Bread"[10] is his prayer that the risen Christ will be revealed in the Lord's Supper in the same way he was with the disciples on the walk to Emmaus (Luke 24:13-35). Although the resurrected Jesus walked and talked with the two disciples, they were unable to recognize him because their perception was blinded by grief over his death. Only when he agreed to stay and eat with them and then blessed the meal were their eyes opened. "Weren't our hearts on fire when he spoke to us along the road and when he explained the scriptures for us?" they asked each other afterward (Luke 24:32 CEB). Propelled by overwhelming joy, they left that same evening, hurrying back to Jerusalem to tell others the good news of Christ's resurrection.

Through all the means of grace, especially the sacrament of the Lord's Supper, John Wesley urges Christians to open ourselves to receive the blessings that God offers and to commit ourselves to obey all of God's commands. The word *obedience* isn't popular in the church today, especially because historically it's been misused by those in power to oppress and subjugate women, children, people of color, and ethnic minorities, all in the name of God. However, the word *obedience* comes from the Latin *oboedire*, which means "listening that leads to action." As we partake of the Lord's Supper, may we come with open hearts and minds, listening and ready to receive what God so lovingly offers. At the Table, in the bread and cup, may we hear Jesus who says to us, I am here for you. Are you here for me?

4

Fasting

As we consider why John Wesley included fasting as means of grace for all time and all people, it is prudent to remember his closing comments in the sermon "The Means of Grace." None of the five means, including fasting, has spiritual merit in and of itself. Each means of grace is but a channel through which God might move. Without a Godward heart, fasting is only a "poor, dead, empty thing: separate from God, it is a dry leaf, a shadow."[1] As we take up the spiritual discipline of fasting in the way of Wesley, then, the appropriate posture is one of humility and openness to God, both to present ourselves vulnerably to God and to open ourselves to receive direction and blessing from God.

The *Didache*, a first-century manual for Christian faith and practice, advises fasting on Wednesdays and Fridays. In his treatise "*De Ieiunio*" (*On Fasting*), theologian Tertullian (155–240 CE) followed suit, recommending fasting on Wednesdays and Fridays from morning until the ninth hour. For these reasons John Wesley, an avid student of the early practices of the church, fasted on Wednesdays and Fridays, breaking his fast with afternoon tea.[2] While the early church had a long list of reasons for fasting, from conquest of bodily appetite to spiritual warfare, there is no command to fast in the New Testament. Jesus was in fact criticized for not making his disciples fast (Matt 9:14-17). However, Jesus did fast in the wilderness as part of his preparation for public ministry.

To understand the purpose of fasting let's consider two narratives from the New Testament. The first story is found in Matthew 17 and Mark 9. Jesus and his inner circle of disciples—Peter, James, and John—have just experienced the extraordinary transfiguration of Jesus on a high mountain. They have seen Moses and Elijah in glorified states, talking with Jesus who is dazzling in white garments. Immediately after the events on the mountain, Jesus and the three return to the valley where the rest of the disciples are exhausted from failed attempts to heal a boy with epilepsy who, according to both accounts, is also demonically oppressed. To make matters worse, a large crowd has gathered and an argument is underway as the legal experts offer their opinions. As he observes the situation, Jesus asks in frustration, "You faithless generation, how long will I be with you? How long will I put up with you? Bring him to me" (Mark 9:19 CEB). Jesus then heals the boy and throws out the unclean spirit. Later, in private, he tells the defeated disciples that "throwing this kind of spirit out requires prayer" (Mark 9:29 CEB). In some ancient manuscripts of Matthew and Mark, Jesus says, "through prayer *and fasting.*" The King James Version of the Bible, which was the standard English translation in Wesley's day, includes the words "and fasting."

The practice of fasting in this story (according to the ancient texts and the King James Version) is linked to both a prayer of discernment and authority over sickness and evil. That is, for some challenges to Christian faith and practice, fasting is an essential element of prayer. Fasting prepares the whole person—body, mind, and spirit—to carry out the missional purposes of God. Fasting literally empties us so that we can be filled with God's spirit of discernment and authority. The story of Jesus's temptation found in Luke 4:1-13 illustrates how fasting prepared him for the launch of his public ministry. Let's enter that story now, with our spiritual senses sharply attuned to what Jesus experiences and why. Using a method of reading Scripture that Ignatius of Loyola, a favorite of John Wesley's, recommends, we will "enter the story" with a "sanctified imagination" as Jesus's companion during his temptation.

As the Spirit drives Jesus into the wilderness, we reluctantly follow our Lord. We don't wish to suffer privation in the wilderness, nor do we wish to learn the true meaning of blessing. We want to name abundance as blessing. Health. Friends. Being without need. But Jesus takes us into the wilderness of extremity, which becomes the Wilderness School of Blessing and Discernment. After many days of hunger, while denied the essential building blocks of life, Jesus's body and mind begin to wither from duress. He is weak, hungry, exhausted, and alone. In this state of extreme privation Satan comes to tempt Jesus. Is he really blessed? Mustn't he now take care of himself since he is clearly on his own?[3]

Jane Lyons of Australia is a renowned artist who painted the temptation in the wilderness in various scenes, all captured on one large panel. Between the scenes she penned the story from Matthew 4:1-11. Satan is very handsome. He looks like Prince Charming in a Disney tale with his ermine-trimmed robe. Jesus, in stark contrast, seems near death. He lies on the ground exhausted in a premonition of his descent from the cross. On his earthen deathbed—deprived of human comfort, food, water, and shelter—Jesus embodies all humanity that groans under impossible poverty. He becomes mothers and children in South Sudan, withering away under the sun because of wartime poverty. He becomes HIV/AIDS patients withering away in loneliness because they have been cut off from family and the hope of a future. Jesus becomes 21 percent of children in the United States who live in the impoverished wilderness where they were born.[4] Jesus suffers in "the least of these," and the lie is always that the blessing has been removed and they're on their own.

We find ourselves asking the question: what must we do? Jane Lyons shows us the answer in her portrayal of the final words of Mark's account. Angels attend to the emaciated Jesus. They wash his feet, comb his hair, bring food and drink. They hold him. They sing to him. They won't let him go. They love him back into wholeness. That's our job—to be the angels who tend to Jesus who is, in the words of Mother Teresa of Calcutta, so often in a distressing disguise. Jesus is found in "the least of these," people who are vulnerable, suffering, disempowered, oppressed, and at the mercy of others. The call to become the angels, the bearers and doers of good news, is the discernment that emerges along the way. The blessing is that we do so not alone but in partnership with God.

Another vocational dimension appears in this Wilderness School of Discernment for Jesus, which is manifest in the timing of the experience. *The Spirit drives Jesus into the wilderness immediately after his baptism and prior to the launch of his ministry.* Jesus heard his heavenly Father say, "This is my Son whom I dearly love; I find happiness in him" (Matt 3:17 CEB). Now he must go into the desert of temptation where his identity as God's dearly loved Son will be tested again and again. It's precisely at the point of great physical need that his spiritual identity comes under attack. If Jesus is to carry out the mission, he must be clear about his identity and able to stand in his authority over and over during opposition from his critics. He must be strong when his disciples are weak. He must be able to discern quickly, from one situation to the next, what is required and what he must do or not do. The temptations in the wilderness prepare him for these challenges.

The journey we take in the wilderness with Jesus is in some ways a template for the journey we always take when we fast. As we enter the emptiness and loneliness of fasting, we increasingly encounter our own vulnerability. Without water, food, and shelter we cannot survive in this world. Even a brief and limited fast, such as Wednesdays and Fridays from morning till late afternoon, brings to our bodily and emotional awareness our constant creaturely need. Despite all the ways we normally behave as if we are in control, we are not. Life is fragile, not to be taken for granted. Fasting is the primary spiritual discipline that brings us back to our vulnerability. Fasting returns us to our deep dependence upon God, which is the fundamental posture of prayer. We are brought into an experience in which we must remember that we, like Jesus, are God's dearly loved sons and daughters. As we bring into prayer the suffering of those for whom we fast, we simultaneously feel our own weakness. We must keep remembering our identity as God's beloved, keep remembering the promises of God, and keep surrendering ourselves to God's care.

Like you, I have experienced complex problems with no clear way forward. During one of these challenges I contacted several friends to ask for prayer, and three immediately promised not only to pray but to fast and pray together until there was a breakthrough. As we exchanged text messages, they reminded each other and me that this kind of problem is resolved through prayer and fasting. Friendship deepened as they leaned into the challenge, trusting God together. I marveled at their love and their spiritual vision. As the days went by, God gave discernment and wisdom. Through it all, my friends continued to fast until resolution came.

Each means of grace empties us of ego and selfishness. During seemingly impossible challenges, the spiritual discipline of fasting truly empties us as we pour ourselves out for others in prayer and faith. Sometimes we might say to a friend, "I will pray. Keep me posted." But sometimes friends do so much more. They give themselves—body, mind, and spirit—to the ministry of fasting and intercession so that God's will might be done, so that you remain grounded as God's dearly loved child during difficult challenges.

Marjorie Thompson describes fasting as a practice of abstinence, not just from food but from activities and attachments that consume our lives, such as social media, television, and the like.[5] In the Epworth Project, the network of new monastic communities administered by the Missional Wisdom Foundation, some houses regularly fast from electronics and social media because abstaining from their devices and the Internet is more challenging than forgoing meals for busy young adults. Time spent without electronics opens space for residents to reorient themselves, to reflect and pray for their neighbors.

Lent is the season in the liturgical year when many Christians practice a sustained fast. In this case fasting is an act of contrition for the ways in which we have failed to live up to the task of following Jesus. Many years ago, when my family and I had just moved to Dallas, Texas, as Lent approached I began to pray about what to "give up for

Lent," which is to say, how I should focus my fast. God spoke to me in an unexpected way, saying that it was time to give up being a hermit in my own neighborhood. As I sputtered internally, I realized that I was a little too fond of the isolation that is possible with high privacy fences and garages. It was easy to not know anyone in my neighborhood. My introverted self liked all that solitude.

That night over dinner I told my family what I was sensing in prayer, and I asked whether they would be open to inviting neighbors for potluck dinners on Tuesdays in March. I hoped they would resist because the idea of cold-calling neighbors to invite them to dinner was about as much fun for me as a painful dental appointment. My heart sank when they said it was a great idea.

So it was that I made a simple invitation that announced Tuesday Dinners in March, with an ethnic theme for each week, including Irish food on the week of Saint Patrick's Day. I put a note at the bottom that we were not selling anything but that we simply wanted to get to know our neighbors. With trepidation I went to each house on our block, inviting people. The first night about fifteen neighbors came. The next week there were even more. On the third week one of our neighbors said she was having so much fun she wanted to continue into the future, only with different houses hosting the meals and moving to a monthly format after March. She pulled out a pen and paper and offered to get people to sign up. The neighborhood potlucks led to the development of real community in our neighborhood, including spiritual friendships for some people. By the time we moved away ten years later, the dinners were still going strong with twenty-five to forty people present each month. Through that experience I learned that when we abstain from an activity, attitude, or practice as a God-breathed spiritual fast, space opens within our hearts and lives for God's creative power. God empties us so that we have room for something new.

In *Celebration of Discipline*, Richard Foster observes, "More than any other Discipline, fasting reveals the things that control us. This is a wonderful benefit to the true disciple who longs to be transformed into the image of Christ. We cover up what is inside us with food and other good things, but in fasting these things surface."[6]

John Wesley taught us that spiritual transformation or growth in holiness not only empowers us for a more meaningful life individually, it also fills us with the Holy Spirit so that we can more fully engage in God's work of making all things new in the world.

5
Christian Conferencing

If you were to ask random people at a shopping mall to define the word *church*, two of the most common answers would be (1) a Sunday morning worship service in a church building, or (2) a church building.

The typical church participant would likely say the same things. These answers aren't exactly wrong, but they aren't right either. The Greek word in the New Testament that we translate "church" is *ekklesia* or "gathering." Jesus said in Matthew 18:20 that wherever two or three are gathered in his name, he is with them. To be "gathered in his name" is to become a group assembled for the express purpose of loving, listening to, following, and participating in the way of Jesus. Being gathered in his name has inward and outward, individual and communal dimensions. This brief description Jesus provides in Matthew 18 is a distillation of what it means to be the church. We are gathered around Jesus, and he is with us. This kind of gathering can and does happen in all sorts of places, including church buildings. At the same time, simply gathering in a church building doesn't guarantee what Jesus means by *ekklesia*. John Wesley makes very clear in his sermon "The Almost Christian" that one can be very religious and spend a lot of time in the church building participating in religious activities without actually being a Christian.[1]

According to Wesley, the chief difference between "almost Christian" and "real Christian" is that real Christians love God and neighbor wholeheartedly. Their faith is lively and transformative in an ongoing way with a steady growth in holiness of heart and life, and their faith is deeply grounded in a living, dynamic relationship with Jesus Christ.

Note well that these characteristics are neither programs nor rituals but loving, honest, practical, relational commitments to God, neighbor, and self. John Wesley's entire theological and ministerial life focused on helping people enter into a dynamic experience of *ekklesia*—Christian community gathered around Jesus for the sake of others. His precedent for this kind of *ekklesia* is the early church, especially as described in the New Testament.

Methodism began with people gathering in exactly the way Jesus described in Matthew 18:20 (which is part of a larger conversation Jesus had with his disciples about how to handle conflict). As a young man, John Wesley started a group called the Holy Club because he and his college friends felt they needed to take much more seriously the claims of Jesus on their lives. They wanted to have a system of accountability for how they were living. In addition to reading the Bible and praying together, they talked about their struggles with temptation and sin, and they helped each other remain active in ministries to people who were in prison and suffering in many other ways. This level of accountability is similar to what happens in a twelve-step group for addiction recovery, such as Alcoholics Anonymous.

After the Methodist movement was underway, John Wesley started small groups called "class meetings" that became the backbone of Methodism.[2] These were small groups facilitated by a class leader, where members followed common spiritual practices and held themselves accountable for how they were attending to all the means of grace. One distinctive of Wesleyan spirituality is the seamless blend of personal and social holiness. Discipleship isn't summed up by attending one hour of worship each week, although corporate worship truly matters as a means of grace. Instead, discipleship is the practice of all the means of grace in every aspect of life.

These smaller groups designed to foster discipleship practices are what John Wesley has in mind when he speaks of "Christian conferencing" as a means of grace. From the time that I experienced Betty's leadership (see chapter 1 on prayer) with the "special ladies," I am firmly convinced that without Christian conferencing it is very difficult to follow Jesus, much less increasingly bear his love and likeness into the world.

There are three essential elements of small groups that foster genuine discipleship or, in Wesley's language, that practice Christian conferencing. These are the following:

1. The group is gathered in the name of Jesus, as described above with regard to Matthew 18:20.

2. The practices of the group foster deep spiritual friendships that lead to growth in personal and corporate holiness and genuine community.

3. The group is engaged in missional ministry beyond itself, thus it is *kenotic* (a Greek word that means "self giving").

Let's look at each of these elements to see why they are essential. As we move through this discussion, think about the best way to introduce Christian conferencing into your congregation, organization, or neighborhood.

Gathered around Jesus

Over several years and along with several friends, I helped establish a network of residential, intentional communities called the Epworth Project. These houses are in diverse social contexts in Dallas, Fort Worth, and Waco and serve as incubators for persons who wish to learn how to live in community, practice a robust fivefold Methodist rule of life,[3] and connect in deeply hospitable, life-giving ways in their neighborhood. Each of the houses is anchored in a church or campus ministry. Most of the residents are young adults, with about half being seminary students.

Over the years, in guiding the houses in their spiritual and justice formation, we learned the first way community houses go off the rails: instead of being gathered around Jesus in order to love, listen to, and follow his way, their center point shifts. Sometimes Jesus at the center is replaced by a conflict or problem relating to the mundane tasks of life, such as washing the dishes or getting up in time for morning prayer. At other times Jesus gets bumped by one of the practices for the rule of life, such as hospitality or fasting! (Legalism is always a temptation for people who choose to take discipleship more seriously.) At those times, it was important to gather the house members and engage in Christian conferencing so that the house could once again center itself around Jesus and his way, with the rule of life as a supportive structure to help the house stay focused and to correct course when hitting inevitable bumps in the road of life together.

The same principle is crucial for marriage, a congregation, or a small group within the church. When we remain centered around Jesus, he is with us and we find our way in participating in his work in the world. Christian conferencing is a means of grace that helps us do that.

Living Out Spiritual Practices

Living with a "rule of life," or set of common spiritual practices, is core to Methodist spirituality. John Wesley was accused by detractors of being a monk, specifically a "closet Jesuit," because of his rule of life and the methodical discipleship system.[4] This is why the derogatory name "Methodist" was a label hurled at Wesley and his friends. Early Methodism was in many ways a lay monastic movement[5] in which the "monastery" was the workaday world of practicing Methodists, especially among the poor and disadvantaged. Their rule of life was distilled in the General Rules. Rueben Job reframed the General Rules in his book *Three Simple Rules*.[6] The original three were the following:

1. First do no harm (similar to the Hippocratic Oath taken by doctors).

2. Do all the good you can.

3. Attend to all the ordinances of God (meaning all the means of grace).

Living by a rule of life isn't meant to be a legalistic or grim adherence to rules and regulations. Rather a rule of life is a set of practices that helps us form habits that are life-giving and liberating for ourselves and others. Wesley would say these habits help us "go on to perfection," by which he means an ever-increasing capacity for love of God and neighbor. When a group practices a common rule of life, one of the richest ways it can experience Christian conferencing is to occasionally have a conversation to focus on reflection questions regarding how it is actually experiencing its rule of life. In the early Methodist movement, a question commonly used in such groups was "How is it with your soul?" Several spiritual friends regularly ask me this question, and they kindly but persistently wait and prod until I answer. I do the same for them. We are able to have this conversation because we love and trust each other, and we keep confidentiality. This kind of mutual conversation, combined with reflection upon scripture and grace-filled prayer for what surfaces in the conversation, goes a long way to shape us into genuine followers of Jesus.

Engaged in Mission

Even so, Christian conferencing isn't complete unless it includes Spirit-breathed action in which the group gives itself to others. Christian conferencing is meant to foster authentic discipleship, which includes both contemplation and action. But how does a group discern the Holy Spirit's leading as to when, where, how, and with whom it will give itself away? What does this look like on the ground?

A few years ago a small group of Christians in Wichita, Kansas, sensed that God was leading them to form a new kind of community in which they would be much more engaged in their neighborhood. Matt and Catherine Johnson lived in one of the roughest neighborhoods in South Central Wichita, and they knew a few of their neighbors. Matt was a staff member at a United Methodist church, and Catherine was a graduate student in environmental studies. Matt and Catherine's friends Adam and Ashley Barlow-Thompson and their toddler, Prescott, lived in a different part of the city and held pastoral positions in two different United Methodist churches.

Over a period of two years these four friends and a few others regularly talked and prayed about their growing sense that God wanted them to enter into a much more intentional way of life that included a change in how they did their ministries and where they all lived. That is, they engaged in Christian conferencing.

As they began meeting with a spiritual director and a missional ministry coach, they learned more about how to listen to the Holy Spirit in community. They grew in their capacity to pay attention to and respect the growing desire God had given them to do a new thing. They began naming their inner resistance to following and trusting God with the new thing. Step by step, they recognized increasingly how God was bringing resources, opportunities, and courage to step out in faith and do the new thing. They were practicing discernment in common, a type of listening prayer.

Finally, they reached a tipping point in listening to and cooperating with the Holy Spirit. Adam, Ashley, and Prescott moved onto the same street as Matt and Catherine. Both couples went for training in Asset-Based Community Development (ABCD) and spent time with Mike Mather, pastor of Broadway United Methodist Church in Indianapolis, which was revolutionized by ABCD. They began practicing community development in their neighborhood, getting to know many of the people living around them and finding out about the gifts, wisdom, dreams, and hopes of their neighbors. They could see that God was already at work in the neighborhood in a number of ways. (In Wesleyan theology we refer to this as *prevenient grace*, or the Holy Spirit's activity among us that helps us experience God and get ready for relationship with God even before we seek or are aware of God.)

Adam, Ashley, Matt, and Catherine learned how to foster networks of opportunities for neighbors to connect with each other so that the neighborhood could flourish in every possible way. As the four friends took each step of obedience (obedience meaning "listening that leads to action"), more steps became clear. They learned by trial and error and by maintaining a sense of humor along the way.

At this writing their ministry is called NeighboringMovement.org and is a hub of beautiful, organic, and transformational living in South Central Wichita.[7] On summer evenings there are front-yard picnics with live music, which they call Fork and Folk. While visiting, I sat in their yard at one of the Fork and Folk events and sang "Yellow Submarine" at the top of my lungs along with an eclectic mob of neighbors. Throughout the year there are craft groups, baking circles, community gardening, recipe swapping, the bartering of skills and tools, and spiritual conversation. Pastoral care. Bible reading. Prayer. Community. An educational program emerged to help churches organically love their actual neighbor as a form of discipleship. The beautiful project is in a constant state of evolution, bearing witness to the dynamism of a life lived as *ekklesia*, a group of friends gathered around Jesus in order to listen to him, love him, and participate with him in the making of all things new.[8]

For NeighboringMovement.org to be born, a small group of Christian friends had to practice Christian conferencing and discernment, and take steps of obedience to give itself away. This process was slow, halting, tearful, sometimes agonizing, sometimes hilarious, and at times misunderstood by skeptical religious onlookers from their own traditions. They didn't have a blueprint or a five-year strategic plan. Nonetheless, the four friends persisted, and are now living into a fresh expression of ministry for experiencing God's love the Wesleyan way.

Becoming a Means of Grace

Throughout this study we considered how and why the five means of grace are so important in the forming of genuine Christian faith and practice. We reflected upon John Wesley's original vision for Christian discipleship and how relevant Methodist spirituality is indeed still evolving for Christians. As we explored each means of grace we noted how it is an expression of prayer that leads to missional engagement. To be a Wesleyan Christian is to be committed to participation in Christ's work of making all things new.

May staying in love with God increasingly compel us through all the means of grace, so that we become a means of grace to our neighbors.

Notes to the Appendix

The Means of Grace Are Spiritual Practices

1. John Wesley, "The Means of Grace," Sermon 16 (1746). Wesley also wrote about the means of grace in the Large Minutes and referenced them in various other texts. For a good summary of Wesley's teaching on the means of grace, see Ted Campbell, "Means of Grace and Forms of Piety" in *The Oxford Handbook on Methodist Studies*, ed. William J. Abraham and James E. Kirby (Oxford: Oxford University Press, 2009), 280–91.

2. Wesley, "The Means of Grace," II.5.

1. Prayer

1. David Keller, *Come and See: The Transformation of Personal Prayer* (New York: Morehouse, 2009), 1.

2. The various streams refer to all the denominations that include the name "Methodist" such as United Methodist, African Methodist Episcopal, and so on. It also refers to traditions that emerged from the nineteenth-century Methodist holiness movement, including the Church of God, various Pentecostal denominations, the Church of the Nazarene, and others.

3. Charles Wesley, "Maker, in Whom We Live," *The United Methodist Hymnal* (Nashville: United Methodist Publishing House, 1989), no. 88.

4. John Wesley, *The Heart of Wesley's Journal*, edited and with an introduction by Robert E. Coleman (New Canaan, CT: Keats Publishing, 1979), 474.

2. Searching the Scriptures

1. Preface, *Explanatory Notes*.

2. Randy Maddox, *Responsible Grace: John Wesley's Practical Theology* (Nashville: Kingswood, 1994), 38.

3. Quoted in Scott J. Jones, *United Methodist Doctrine: The Extreme Center* (Nashville: Abingdon, 2002), 130.

4. Preface to *Explanatory Notes of the Old Testament*.

5. For an in-depth treatment of *Lectio Divina,* including five hundred passages of scripture with which to pray using *Lectio*, see Thelma Hall, *Too Deep for Words: Rediscovering Lectio Divina* (Mahwah, NJ: Paulist Press, 1988).

6. This phrase is the title of Robert Mulholland's book on reading the Bible for spiritual transformation, *Shaped by the Word: The Power of Scripture in Spiritual Formation*, rev. ed. (Nashville: Upper Room, 2001).

3. The Lord's Supper

1. The Bruderhoff are a network of more than two thousand intentional communities that began in Germany in 1920 and now exist on four continents. For more about their history, faith, and service, see http://www.bruderhof.com/?gclid=CjwKEAjwu4_JBRDpgs2RwsCbt 1MSJABOY8an4vT53AOFqnqPh85GwbaODOhRwxnLC-87rQ7N 9jDhHxoCJrXw_wcB.

2. A Christian intentional community is a group of persons who live together or near each other, who follow common spiritual practices such as prayer and hospitality as a means of bearing the love of God into the world together.

3. Wesley, "The Means of Grace," II.1.

4. *United Methodist Hymnal*, 33–44.

5. *United Methodist Hymnal*, 14.

6. Henri J. M. Nouwen, *Life of the Beloved: Spiritual Living in a Secular World*, 10th anniversary edition (New York: Crossroad, 2014).

7. *United Methodist Hymnal*, 12.

8. Sara Miles, *Take This Bread: A Radical Conversion* (New York: Ballantine, 2008).

9. The Apostle Paul encountered the living Christ on the Damascus Road, shattering all his former certainty about God and converting him to the faith he once persecuted. For the story of Paul's conversion, see Acts 9.

10. *United Methodist Hymnal*, no. 613.

4. Fasting

1. Wesley, "The Means of Grace," sermon 16, 1746.

2. Campbell, "Means of Grace and Forms of Piety," 287.

3. A brief version of part of this reflection on the temptation of Jesus previously appeared in a Facebook Lenten reflection I posted on March 2, 2017.

4. "Child Poverty," National Center for Children in Poverty, http://www.nccp.org/topics/childpoverty.html.

5. Marjorie Thompson, *Soul Feast: An Invitation to the Christian Spiritual Life* (Louisville: Westminster John Knox, 1995), 76.

6. Richard J. Foster, *Celebration of Discipline: The Path to Spiritual Growth*, revised and expanded (San Francisco: Harper & Row, 1988), 55.

5. Christian Conferencing

1. John Wesley, "The Almost Christian," sermon 2.

2. For good recent guides to forming class meetings and other kinds of covenant groups in the Wesleyan tradition in the twenty-first century,

see Steven W. Maskar, *Disciples Making Disciples: A Guide for Covenant Discipleship Groups and Class Leaders* (Nashville: Discipleship Resources, 2016); and Kevin Watson, *A Blueprint for Discipleship: Wesley's General Rules as a Guide for Christian Living* (Nashville: Discipleship Resources, 2009).

3. Prayers, Presence, Gifts, Service, and Witness. Under each of these five rubrics there are several concrete practices. A set of reflection questions guides practitioners through reflection in a truly Wesleyan process similar to a class meeting.

4. The Jesuits, or Society of Jesus, was founded by Ignatius of Loyola in the fifteenth century. See http://www.ignatianspirituality.com/ignatian -voices/st-ignatius-loyola.

5. Don't let the word *monastic* throw you off. For a good introduction to new expressions of old monasticism, see Jonathan Wilson-Hartgrove, *New Monasticism: What It Has to Say to Today's Church* (Grand Rapids: Brazos, 2008). For specifically Methodist contexts, see Elaine A. Heath and Scott T. Kisker, *Longing for Spring: A New Vision for Wesleyan Community* (Eugene, OR: Cascade, 2010).

6. Rueben P. Job, *Three Simple Rules: A Wesleyan Way of Living* (Nashville: Abingdon, 2010). This small-group study is the first in a foundation series that includes this book, *Five Means of Grace*, as well as *Five Marks of a Methodist* by Steve Harper and *One Faithful Promise* by Magrey deVega.

7. SoCe Life, http://www.socelife.org/.

8. See Revelation 21:5.

CPSIA information can be obtained
at www.ICGtesting.com
Printed in the USA
LVOW13s1939050817
543884LV00006B/7/P